Penguin Handbooks
Simple Knitting

Maj-Britt Engström was born in 1942 and studied as a
textile stylist at the Göteborg School of Applied Art
(1970–74). She has worked mainly in weaving (much of
her work is designed to hang up in offices and waiting
rooms) and she has knitted, woven and embroidered
products for the Swedish Home Craft Association.
Maj-Britt Engström has also shown her work at
many exhibitions.

MAJ-BRITT ENGSTRÖM

SIMPLE
KNITTING

Translated from the Swedish by
Päivi and Peter Crofts

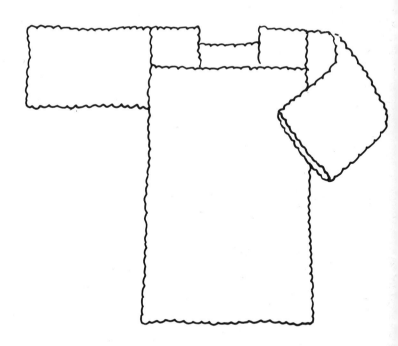

PENGUIN BOOKS

Penguin Books Ltd, Harmondsworth,
Middlesex, England
Penguin Books, 625 Madison Avenue,
New York, New York 10022, U.S.A.
Penguin Books Australia Ltd, Ringwood,
Victoria, Australia
Penguin Books Canada Ltd, 2801 John Street,
Markham, Ontario, Canada L3R 1B4
Penguin Books (N.Z.) Ltd, 182–190 Wairau Road,
Auckland 10, New Zealand

First published by Bokförlaget Prisma Stockholm 1975
Published in Penguin Books 1978
Copyright © Maj-Britt Engström, 1975
This translation copyright © Penguin Books Ltd, 1977
Figures on pages 9, 10 and 12 copyright © Penguin Books Ltd, 1977
All rights reserved

Made and printed in Great Britain by
Butler & Tanner Ltd, Frome and London
Set in Monophoto Ehrhardt

Contents

Foreword

Knitting has always been a popular craft, and is now more popular than ever. In the past people learnt to knit from each other; different designs and ways of knitting were handed down through a family or regional tradition. Today we buy a pattern with the yarn already worked out – we have almost completely abandoned our ability to choose a yarn, colour and style for a garment.

This book gives knitters an opportunity to carry out their own ideas. The general instructions starting on page 7 apply to all garments in the book. Some garments also have further instructions. Each garment is made from straight pieces. All you need to know is how to cast on, how to do garter stitch and how to cast off. And even for these, the book gives simple instructions.

Good luck!

MAJ–BRITT ENGSTRÖM

General instructions

Choosing yarn and knitting needles

For some garments we suggest the type of yarn and size of knitting needle to be used. All measurements on the pattern diagrams are in centimetres. Because stitch tensions differ from person to person you must first find out how many stitches you knit to the centimetre. To do this knit a sample piece.

Cast on 20–40 stitches (a few stitches with thick yarn and large needles; more stitches with fine yarn and needles) making the trial piece is at least 10 cm wide. Knit until the panel is 5–10 cm long. Check that the tension is correct if the knitting seems too loose change to finer needles (lower number); if it looks too tight change to larger needles (higher number).

Lay the knitting out on a flat surface, insert two pins, 10 cm from each other. Now count the number of stitches between the pins, divide this number by 10 and you will have the number of stitches per centimetre.

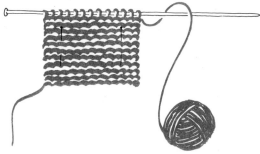

Example: if, using thick wool and 5 mm knitting needles you have knitted 15 stitches to the 10 cm, then for 1 cm you will need 1·5 stitches.

The hat on page 18 is 36 cm round the brim. That means casting on 36 × 1·5 stitches, i.e. 54 stitches. The front of the child's sweater on page 26 is 23 cm – so you cast on 23 × 1·5=34·5 stitches, which you should round up to 35 stitches.

By changing the tension as well as the type of yarn, you can vary the look of a garment. If you knit a fine wool with large needles you will achieve an open-work effect. Or you can combine a rough yarn in some parts of the garment with a fine one in others. You can also mix mohair or bouclé yarns with plain wool and get an interesting textured surface.

Knitting the garments

Turn to a page with a pattern diagram. The measurement required for casting on is given below the double line on each pattern piece. (All measurements are in centimetres.) Knit plain in garter stitch – every row knitted. Work in the direction of the arrow; when you have knitted about 5 cm check that the width has remained the same. Increase number of stitches to widen the piece; to narrow it, decrease.

Making up the garments

If you wish to have the knitted pieces even and smooth before joining them, either wash them and then leave to dry on a flat surface, or lay a damp cloth over the knitted pieces and on top of this a wad of paper. Leave overnight. Peel off the paper and cloth and leave the knitting until dry.

Never put a hot iron directly on to a garment knitted in garter stitch: it may lose its original texture.

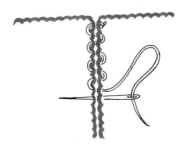

Before sewing up a garment put in any necessary gathering thread (using the yarn you have been knitting with). Then pin the pieces together so that A comes against A, B against B, and so on. Sew. Use simple stitches (as shown above). Do not pull the thread very hard; check that the tension of the seam is equal to that of the garment.

When attaching a cuff to a sleeve you will see that the pieces are different widths. To avoid losing elasticity in the seam stretch out the cuff, pin it carefully to fit the sleeve and then sew them together.

Casting on

There are several ways of casting on. Here is one of the simplest.

1. Make a slip loop in the end of the yarn, put it onto one of the needles, and pull tight.
2. Hold this first needle in your left hand. Hold the other needle in your right hand. Slip the right-hand needle into the loop on the left-hand needle, from front to back. Wind the yarn in your right hand under the right-hand needle and then over the top of it.
3. Pull the loop made in this way through the first stitch on the left-hand needle, then slip the loop onto this needle to make a new stitch. Place the right-hand needle into this new loop and continue as before until you have as many stitches as you need.

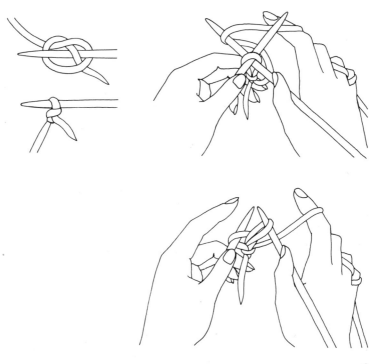

Garter stitch

Garter stitch consists of rows of plain knitted stitches.

1. Hold the needle with the cast-on stitches in your left hand. Hold the other needle with the yarn round the fingers of your right hand as shown below.
2. Pass the tip of the right-hand needle through the first stitch on the left-hand needle, going from front to back. Pass the yarn under and then over the top of the right-hand needle.
3. Pull the loop made in this way through the first stitch on the left-hand needle.
4. Keep this newly made stitch on the right-hand needle, allowing the old stitch through which it has been pulled to slip off the left-hand needle. Move on to the next stitch.

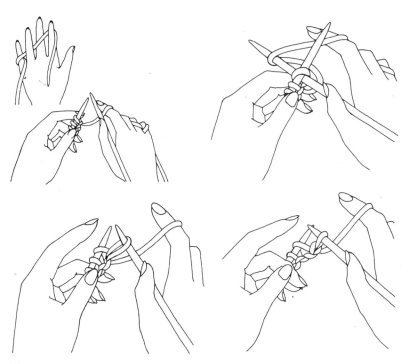

Carry on in this way until you reach the end of the row when all the stitches will have moved onto the right-hand needle. To knit the next row, swap the two needles round in your hands so that the right-hand needle with all the stitches moves to your left hand, and vice versa. Start the next row. Try to keep the knitting neither too loose nor too tight, and of an even tension.

Casting off

1. Knit the first two stitches of the row. You now have two stitches on the right-hand needle. Push the tip of the left-hand needle into the first of the two stitches, i.e. the one at the edge of the knitting.
2. Lift this stitch up over the second stitch and allow it to drop off the needle. Knit another stitch, lift the outside stitch over it, and allow it to drop off.

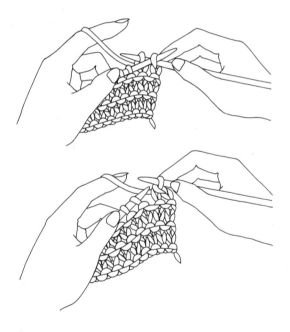

Carry on like this until you have cast off as many stitches as you want to. If you are casting off the whole piece of knitting, break off the yarn after casting off the second-to-last stitch and then pull it through the last stitch so that the stitch is firmly held. You can also cast off stitches in the middle of a piece of knitting if you need to make a slit or other kind of opening.

Think...

...this is a book of ideas. The materials and equipment mentioned are only examples and all the examples are in plain knitting. The amounts of yarn needed are calculated approximately. Use your imagination, together with the general instructions, for further ideas.

Key to the patterns

Casting-on line.

Folded edge.

Measurement between two points: 10 cm.

Line of fringe.

Instead of casting off, knit together every two stitches on the last row and then pull a piece of yarn through the stitches to form a wavy gather.

A   Letters indicating the pieces of garment to match up before sewing.

Gather.

See page 26: 'reducing lines'.

Decoration

Edgings are one of the simplest and yet most effective and varied ways of decorating a garment. You can also embroider your knitting, using cross stitch, chain stitch and knots to make bands of little motifs or figures. See the suntop on pages 66 and 67.

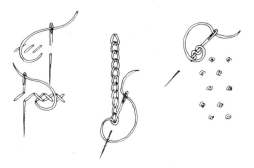

Changes of yarn within a piece of knitting produce different inside and outside surfaces, either of which may be used as the outside of a garment. In the child's top on page 50, one side of the knitting is showing, in the jacket on page 76 the other. These effects can also be mixed in the same garment.

Other good ways of decorating are to crochet round the edges, sew on a piece of braid or a pretty button, tie on a fringe, or use a seam as a feature and embroider on it with crowsfoot stitch or blanket stitch.

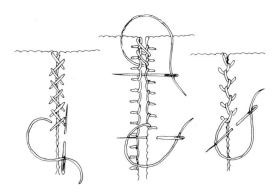

Hat

Size: Adult. For children reduce the pattern.
Yarn: Preferably thick, soft, fluffy yarn.
Amount required: 2–3 × 50 g.
Note: To make a more close-fitting hat reduce the casting-on edge and then just fold it up.

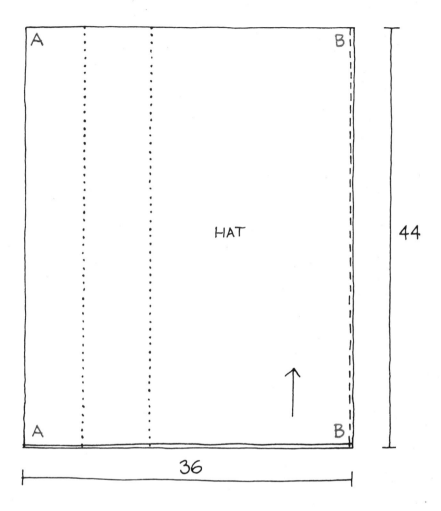

A   B

HAT

A   B

44

36

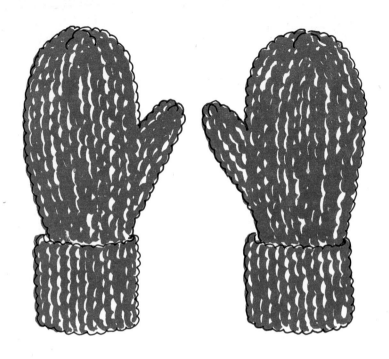

Mittens

Size: For children 10–12 years (above) and small adults (below). To change the size, measure your hand and alter the pattern accordingly.
Yarn: Use any yarn.
Amount required: 2–3 × 50 g.
Note: You can vary the length of the cuffs.

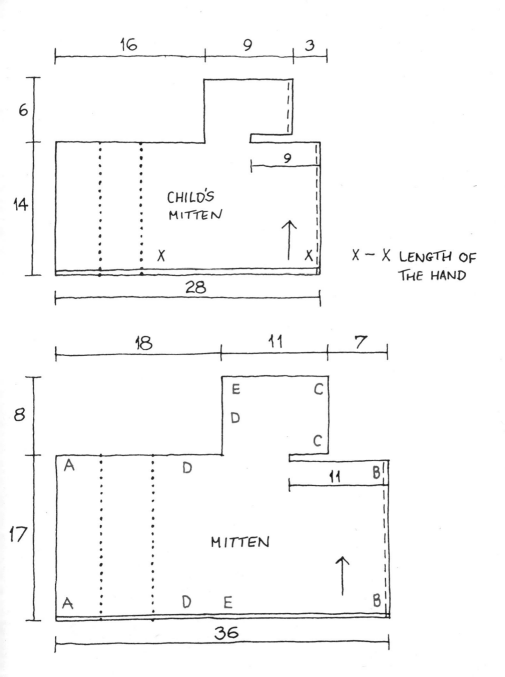

16   9   3

6

14

CHILD'S
MITTEN

9

X   X

X — X LENGTH OF
THE HAND

28

18   11   7

8

17

E   C

D

C

A   D

B

11   B

MITTEN

A   D   E   B

36

Socks

Size: Shoe size $6\frac{1}{2}$–8 (continental 40–42). It is easy to alter the pattern for smaller or bigger feet.
Yarn: Use any yarn.
Amount required: 3–5 × 50 g.
Note: Leather soles can be sewn on these socks.

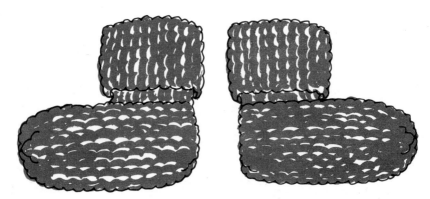

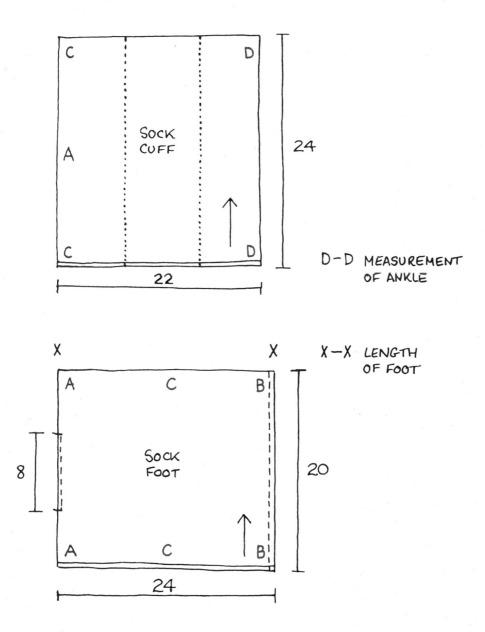

C   D

A   SOCK
      CUFF   24

C   D

22

D—D MEASUREMENT
       OF ANKLE

X   X   X—X LENGTH
                            OF FOOT

A   C   B

8   SOCK
      FOOT   20

A   C   B

24

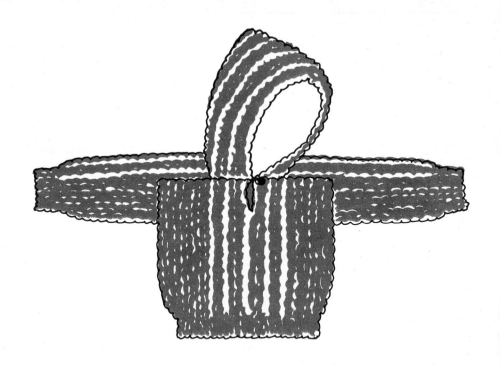

Child's sweater with hood

Size: For a one-year-old. For other sizes see the chart, pages 92–3.
Yarn: Thick and fluffy yarn, suitable for no. 5 needles. You may also use thinner yarns.
Amount required: 5–6 × 50 g.
Note: The jacket top can be made without the hood if you don't have enough yarn. You can knit a collar or edging instead.
Special description of 'reducing line': On the back, front and sleeve pieces in the pattern there is a wavy line. This is the 'reducing line'. Beyond this point the knit becomes tighter yet more elastic, like stocking stitch. See page 25 where the white stripes stop at the 'reducing line'. To make this, stop short of the end of every third row and turn back without knitting the last few stitches, only knitting them when you reach the next row.

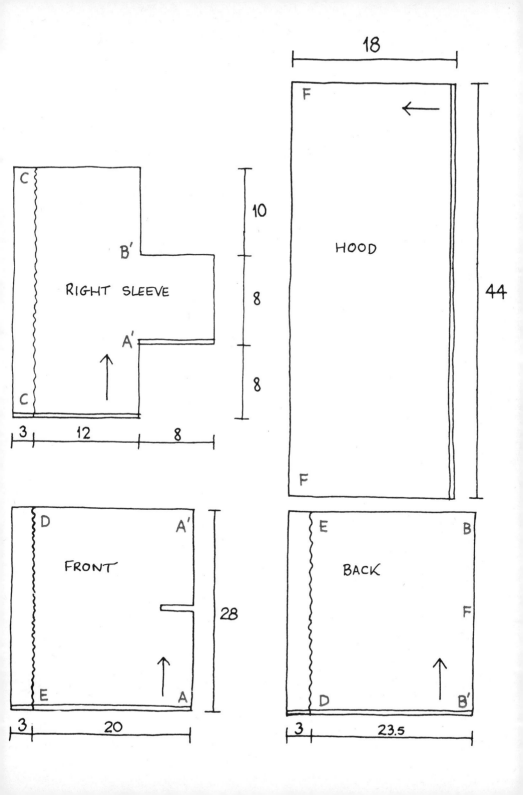

Sweater

Size: Medium man's size 38–40. For other sizes see the chart on pages 92–3.

Yarn: Choose as you please, bearing in mind that this is a large garment. A light, fluffy yarn is the warmest and will not make the sweater too heavy.

Amount required: 18–22 × 50 g.

Special instructions: See page 26.

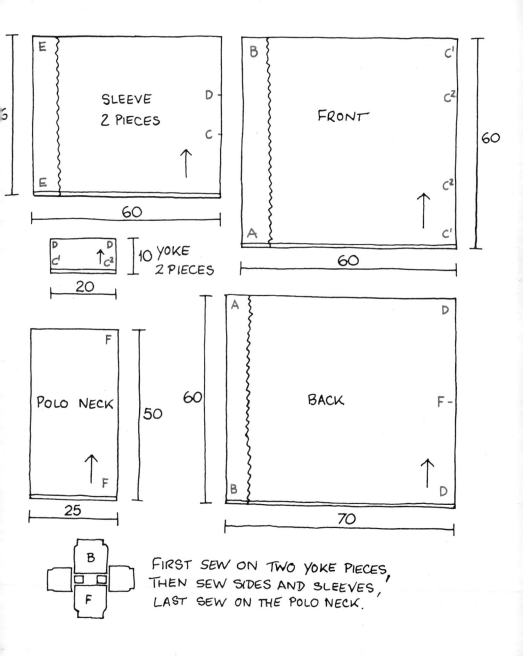

E

SLEEVE
2 PIECES

D ⊣
C ⊣

E

60

B
C¹

FRONT

C²

C²

A
C¹

60

60

D D
C¹ C²

] 10 YOKE
2 PIECES

20

F

POLO NECK

50

F

25

A
D

60

BACK

F ⊣

B
D

70

B

F

FIRST SEW ON TWO YOKE PIECES,
THEN SEW SIDES AND SLEEVES,
LAST SEW ON THE POLO NECK.

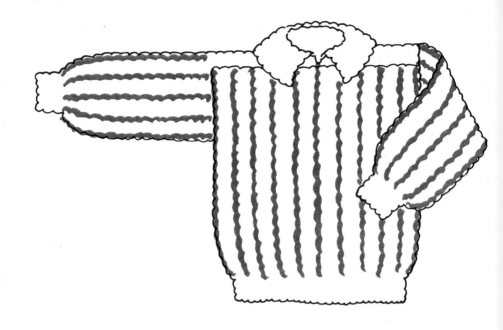

Sweater with a collar

Size: Women's size 14. For other sizes see the chart on pages 92–3.
Yarn: All types suitable.
Amount required: 16–20 × 50 g.
Special instructions: See page 26.

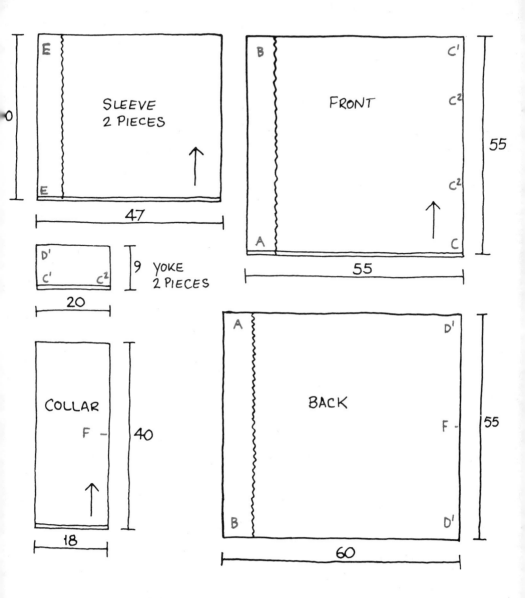

SLEEVE
2 PIECES

E

E

47

0

YOKE
2 PIECES

D'
C'   C²

20

9

FRONT

B

C'

C²

C²

A

C

55

55

COLLAR

F -

40

18

BACK

A

D'

B

D'

F -

55

60

31

Polo-neck collar

Size: Fits most adults. Reduce the size for children according to their measurements.
Yarn: All types suitable.
Amount required: 2–4 × 50 g.

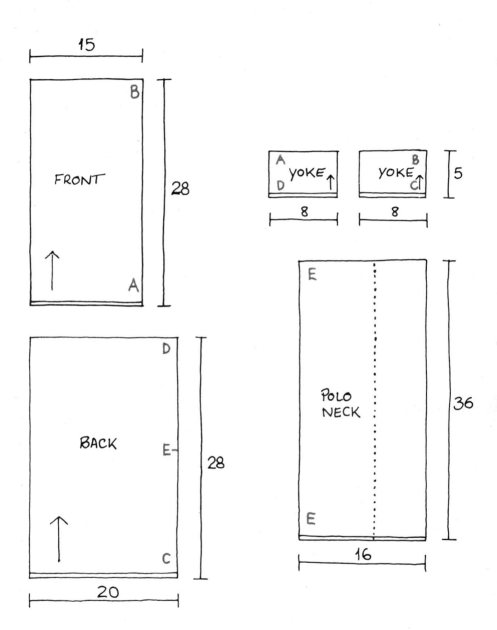

15

B

FRONT

28

A

D

BACK

E

C

28

20

A YOKE
D

B YOKE
C

5

8

8

E

POLO
NECK

36

E

16

33

Scarf hat

Size: Fits most people, but for children under 5 you need to reduce the measurements.

Yarn: Use an elastic type of yarn to make the garment warmer and more comfortable to wear. The scarf hat on page 36 has been knitted with 2-ply yarn, the type generally used for weaving and rug-making, with size 10 needles. The garment has then been washed and brushed when dry in order to make it soft and woolly.

Amount required: 4–5 × 50 g.

Special instructions: The dotted lines on the pattern indicate the place for the fringe. Each time you come to this mark make a 30 cm long loop. On the next row do the same again and then cut all the loops in the middle; knot them securely with the loops in the previous row.

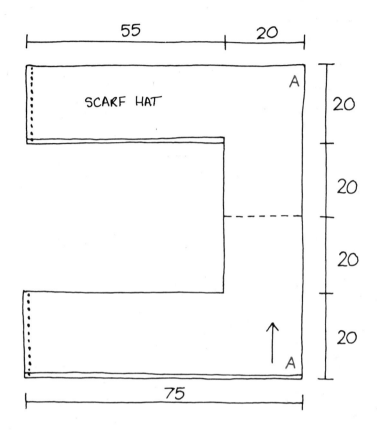

SCARF HAT

55 | 20
75

20
20
20
20

A

A

Child's socks

Size: 1–3 years, see the pattern.
Yarn: Stretchy, thin yarn if the socks are to be worn inside boots or shoes. Use a rough and hard-wearing type if they are for moccasins with leather soles. For the socks on page 37 we used size 12 needles.
Amount required: 1–2 × 50 g.
Special instructions: The mark at the top of the sock pattern is the 'reducing line' – see page 26.

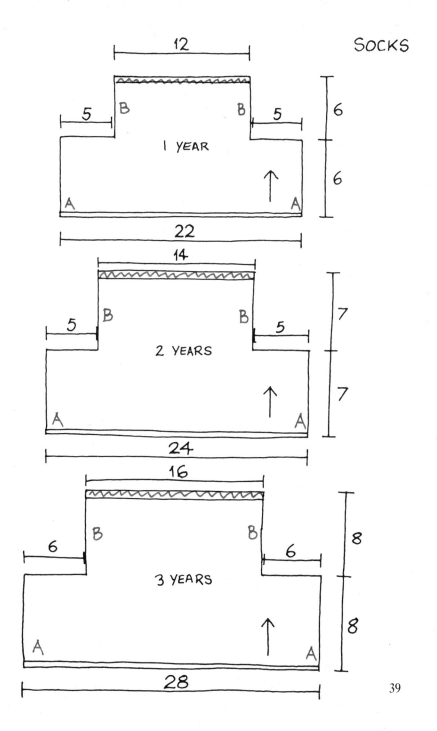

SOCKS

12

5 B   B 5

6

1 YEAR

6

A   A

22

14

5 B   B 5

7

2 YEARS

7

A   A

24

16

B   B

8

6   6

3 YEARS

8

A   A

28

Child's mittens

Size: 1–3 years, see the pattern.
Yarn: All types suitable. You can use a rough woolly yarn for the hand piece and a more elastic one for the cuff. For the mittens on page 37 we used size 12 needles.
Amount required: 1–2 × 50 g.
Special instructions: For the marks at the top of the pattern, see explanation on page 26.

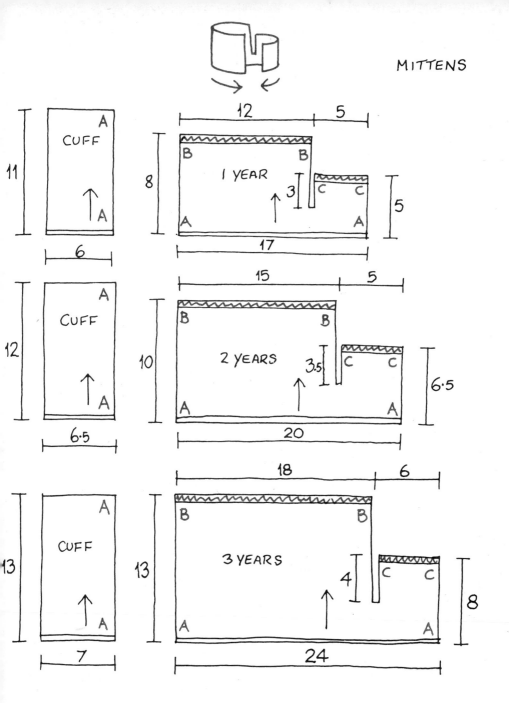

MITTENS

41

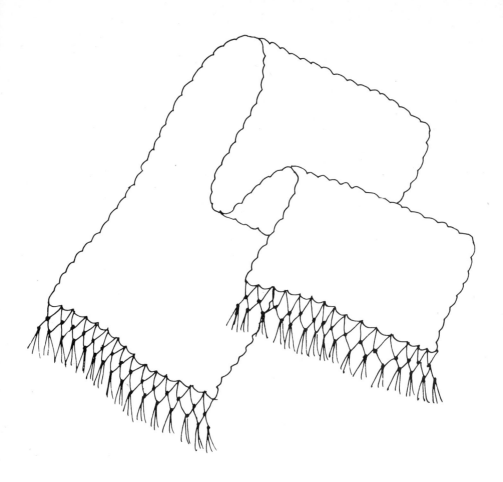

Shawl

All types of yarn are suitable. A shawl made with relatively thin yarn but with large needles can be just as warm as a tightly knitted one.
Amount required: 4–6 × 50 g, depending on the tension of the knitting.

42

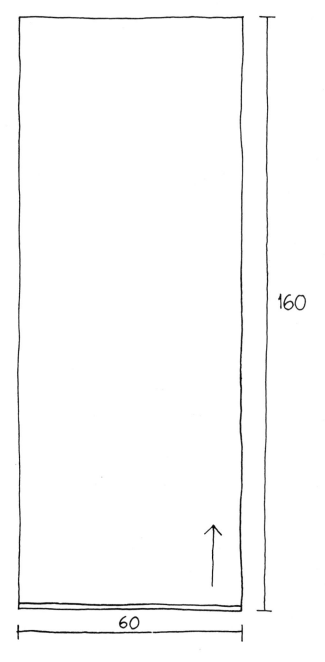

160

60

43

Scarf

Making a scarf is a good way to use up odd bits of yarn. You can mix different qualities and vary the texture by using bigger and smaller needles in turn. You can even knit small patches and sew them together.

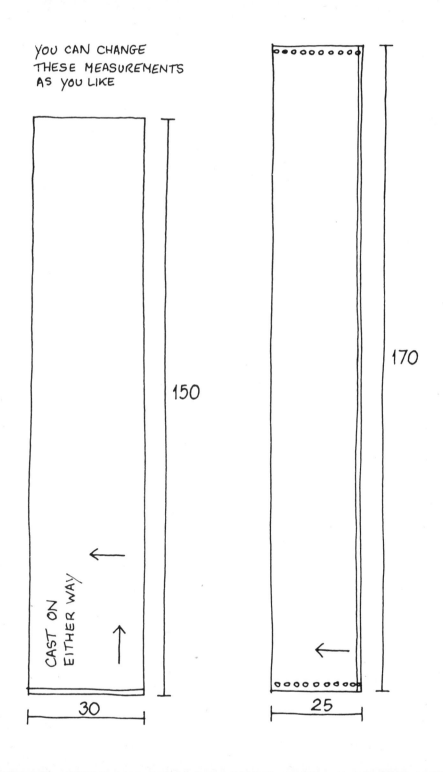

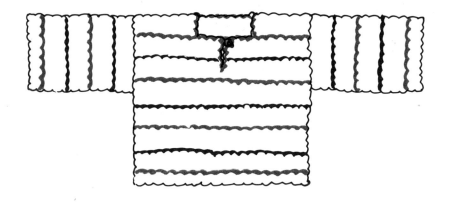

Child's top

Size: 0–2 years. See the patterns on the three following pages.
Yarn: All types suitable. The top on page 50 has been made with light-weight cotton yarn on no. 11 needles. This makes it easy to wash.
Amount required: 3–6 × 50 g.
Note: The stripes on this design are made by two rows of knitting, thus the inside and outside of each part look different and you can choose which side to use.

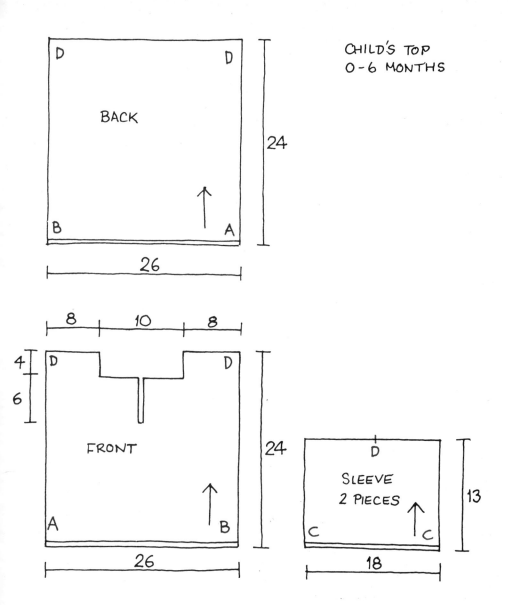

CHILD'S TOP
0-6 MONTHS

BACK

24

26

8 | 10 | 8

4

6

FRONT

24

26

SLEEVE
2 PIECES

13

18

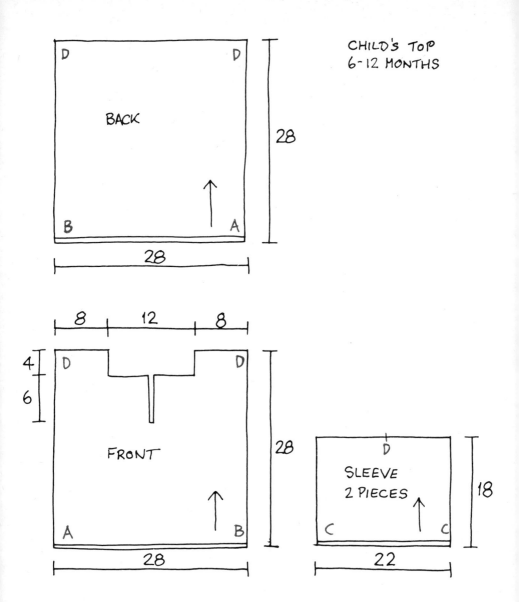

CHILD'S TOP
6-12 MONTHS

BACK
28
28

FRONT
8 12 8
4
6
28
28

SLEEVE
2 PIECES
18
22

48

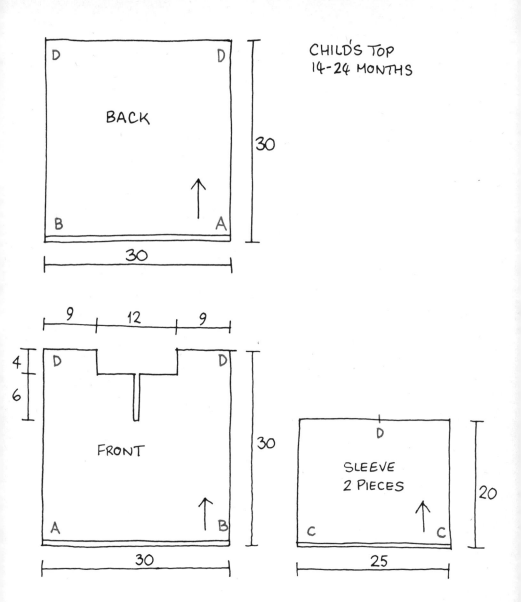

CHILD'S TOP
14-24 MONTHS

BACK

D   D

B   A

30

30

9   12   9

4

6

FRONT

D   D

A   B

30

30

SLEEVE
2 PIECES

D

C   C

25

20

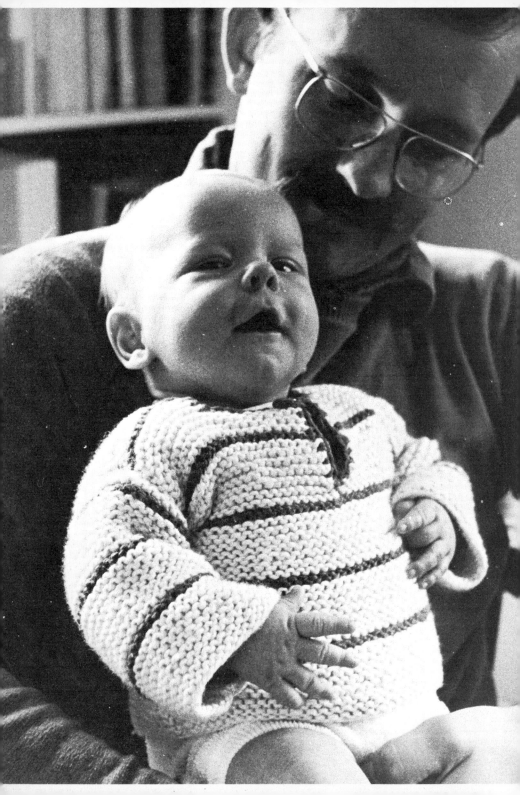

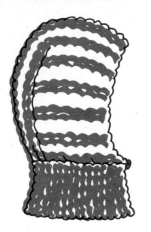

Child's helmet

Size: 1–3 years, see pattern.
Yarn: All types suitable.
Amount required: 2–3 × 50 g.
Note: The neck edges should not be sewn together but fastened with buttons or Velcro.

52

HELMET

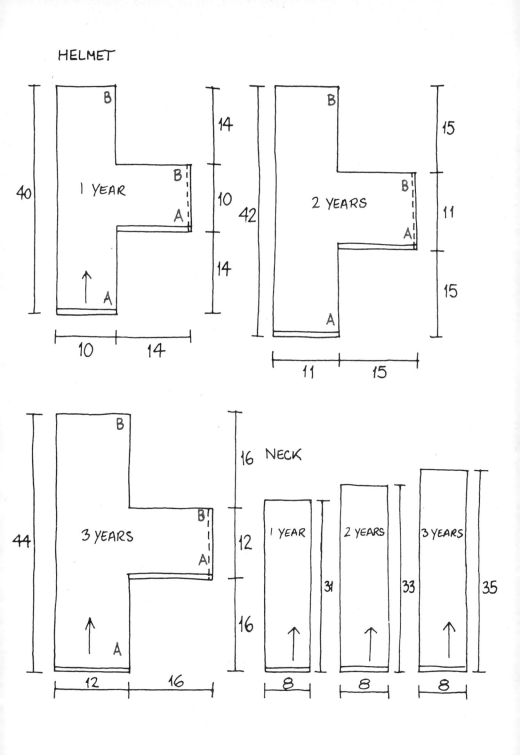

Sleeping-bag

Size: 6 months.
Yarn: Thick and fluffy, needs to be knitted tightly; if the knitting is loose the bag will need lining.
Amount required: 7–10 × 50 g.
Note: The bottom can be sewn up or fastened with a zip. The bag can also be made without sleeves.

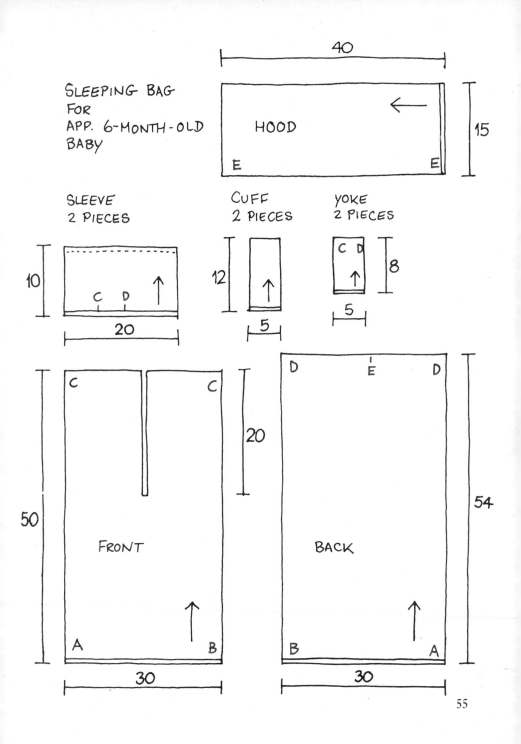

SLEEPING BAG
FOR
APP. 6-MONTH-OLD
BABY

40

HOOD

15

E   E

SLEEVE
2 PIECES

10

C   D

20

CUFF
2 PIECES

12

5

YOKE
2 PIECES

C D

8

5

C   C

20

50

FRONT

A   B

30

D   E   D

BACK

54

B   A

30

55

Sweater with cross-over collar

Size: Women's size 12–14. If you wish to increase or reduce the measurements, cut out the pattern pieces in paper or calico a few centimetres bigger or smaller according to your requirements and try them on.

Yarn: All types suitable. The jumper can be made either for light indoor or heavier outdoor wear.

Amount required: 14–16 × 50 g.

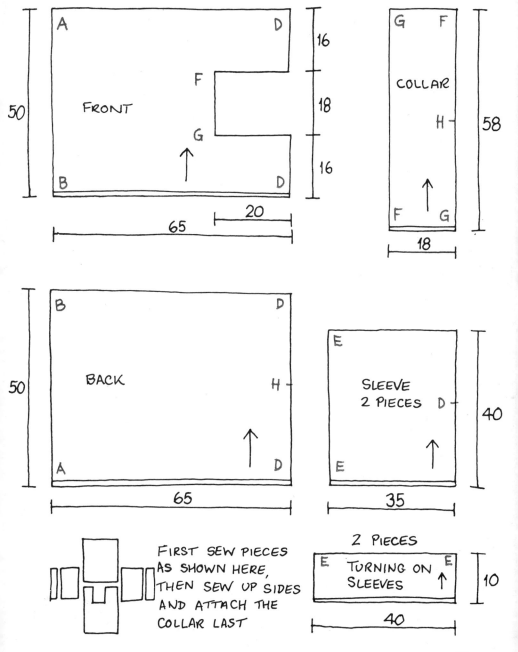

FRONT — A, D, F, G, B, D — 50, 16, 18, 16, 65, 20

COLLAR — G, F, H, F, G — 58, 18

BACK — B, D, H, A, D — 50, 65

SLEEVE 2 PIECES — E, D, E — 40, 35

2 PIECES TURNING ON SLEEVES — E, E — 10, 40

FIRST SEW PIECES AS SHOWN HERE, THEN SEW UP SIDES AND ATTACH THE COLLAR LAST

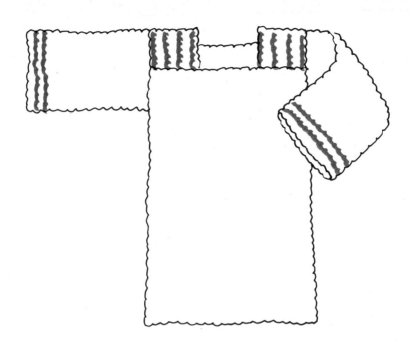

Dress

Size: Medium, women's size 14. For alterations see pages 92–3. Remember that the chart is made for tops and that the dress has a lower neckline.

Yarn: Thin cotton or similar yarns are best for a summer dress. For a winter dress you can use thicker yarns. To avoid stretching, the dress should not be made too heavy.

Amount required: 18–20 × 50 g.

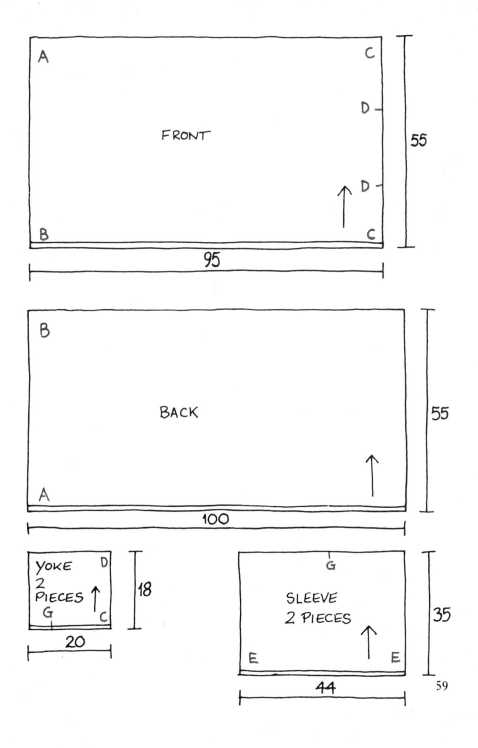

FRONT

A   C

D

D

B   C

55

95

BACK

B

A

55

100

YOKE
2
PIECES

D

G   C

18

20

SLEEVE
2 PIECES

G

E   E

35

44

59

Summer dress

Size: Medium women's. To alter the size, the measurement of the band B–B (about 70 cm) is the most important one. For a good hang, fit the band to your measurements.
Yarn: For instructions see page 58.
Amount required: 16–18 × 50 g.

THESE BANDS MAY BE CAST ON FROM EITHER END

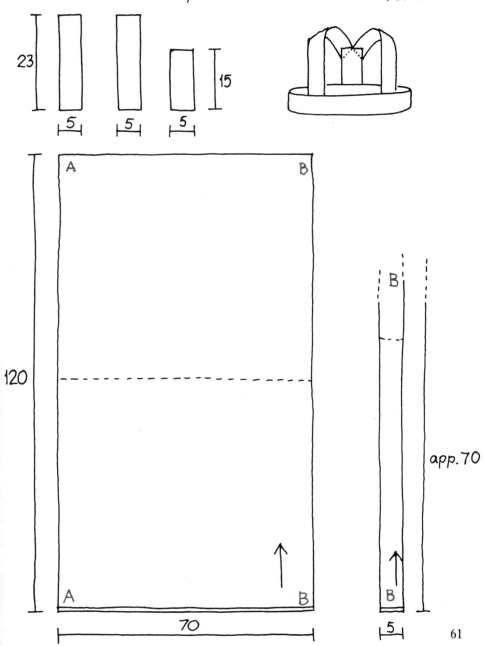

23

15

5 5 5

A   B

120

70

A   B

B

app. 70

B

5

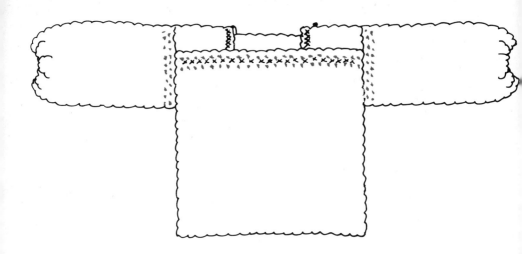

Blouse

Size: 12–14 years. For alterations see chart on pages 92–3.
Yarn: To achieve a cool and airy effect use thin cotton or other similar yarns with big needles.
Amount required: 6–8 × 50 g.
Note: This garment is ideally suited for decoration. You can, for example, use crochet, or thread a decorative cord around the neck, or gather wrists with elastic thread.

BLOUSE
FOR A 12-14-YEAR-OLD

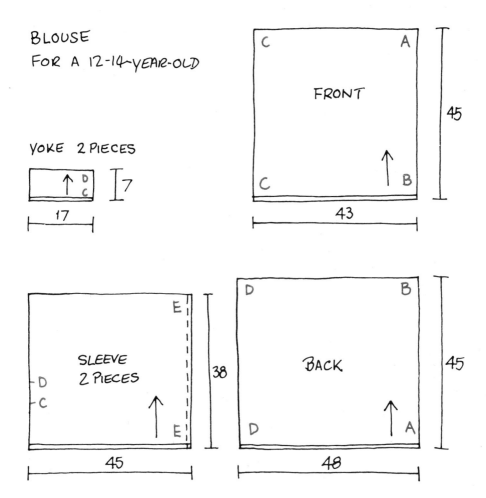

YOKE 2 PIECES

17

7

D
C

FRONT

C   A

C   B

45

43

SLEEVE
2 PIECES

E

D
C

E

45

38

BACK

D   B

D   A

45

48

Sloppy Joe

Size: 14.
Yarn: All types suitable.
Amount required: 16–18 × 50 g.
Note: The gussets under the arm are not necessary, but they make the sweater more roomy.

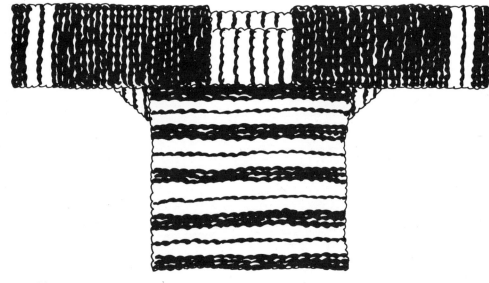

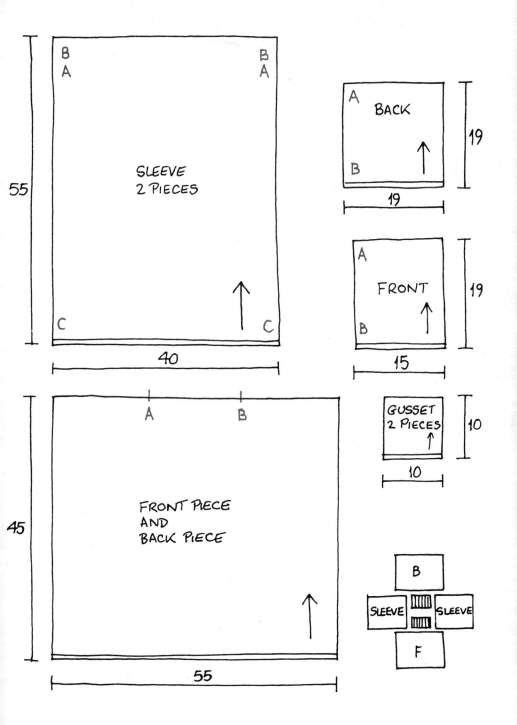

B
A

B
A

SLEEVE
2 PIECES

55

C

C

40

A   BACK

19

B

19

A

FRONT

19

B

15

A   B

FRONT PIECE
AND
BACK PIECE

45

55

GUSSET
2 PIECES

10

10

B

SLEEVE   SLEEVE

F

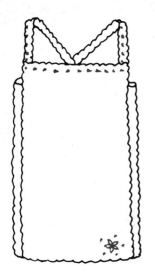 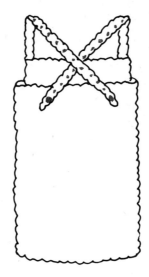

Suntop or vest

Size: 10–12 years.
Yarn: Use cotton or similar yarn and small needles – size 12.
Amount required: 3–4 × 50 g.
Note: To keep the shape knit quite tightly.

SHOULDER-STRAPS 2 PIECES

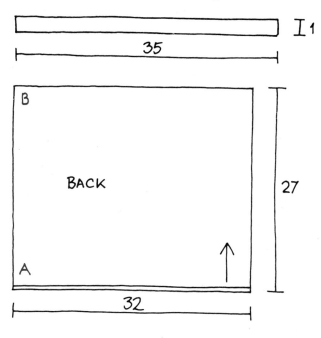

35

I 1

B

BACK

27

A

32

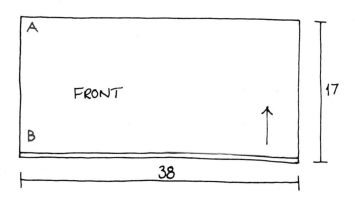

A

FRONT

17

B

38

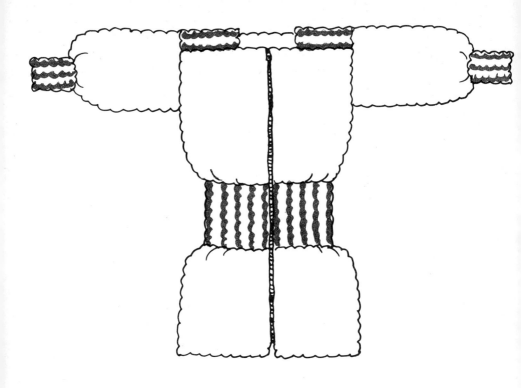

Jacket

Size: Women's size 12.
Yarn: All types suitable. Use double yarn for all parts except the cuffs and yoke where the yarn should be single.
Amount required: 18–20 × 50 g.

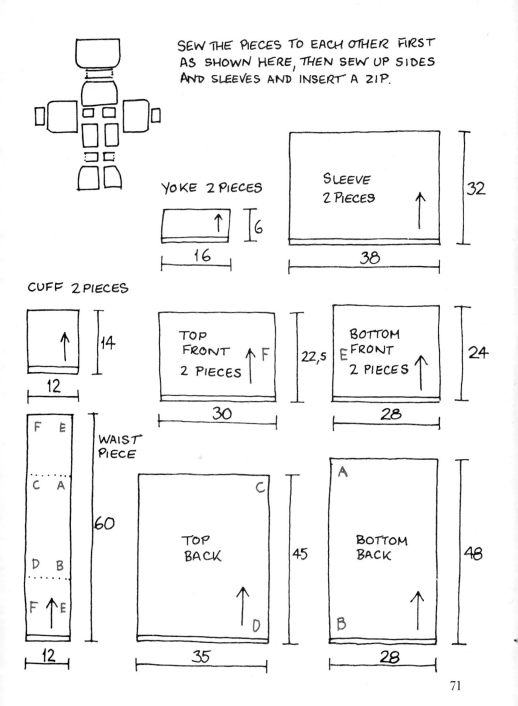

SEW THE PIECES TO EACH OTHER FIRST
AS SHOWN HERE, THEN SEW UP SIDES
AND SLEEVES AND INSERT A ZIP.

YOKE 2 PIECES

16 · 6

SLEEVE
2 PIECES

32

38

CUFF 2 PIECES

14

12

TOP
FRONT
2 PIECES   F

22,5

30

BOTTOM
FRONT
2 PIECES   E

24

28

WAIST
PIECE

F E

C A

D B

F E

60

12

TOP
BACK

C

D

45

35

BOTTOM
BACK

A

B

48

28

71

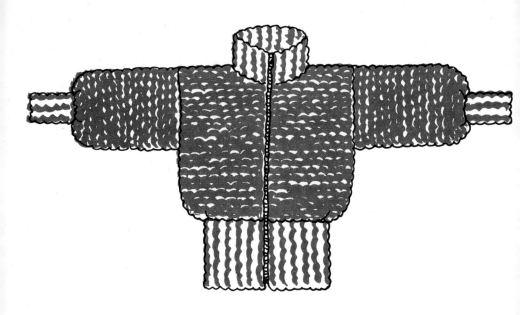

Short jacket

Size: 8–14 years. See patterns on the following three pages.
Yarn: All types suitable. For the front and back use rough and woolly yarn, softer for collar and cuffs.
Amount required: 9–10 × 50 g.

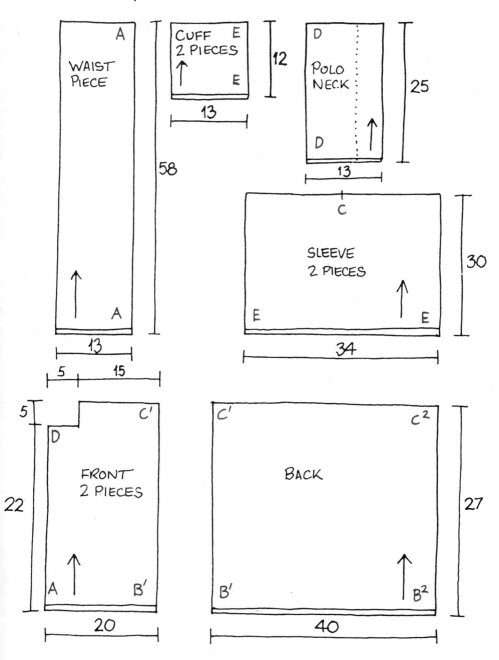

SIZE 8-9 YEARS

WAIST PIECE — A, A — 58, 13, 5, 15

CUFF 2 PIECES — E, E — 12, 13

POLO NECK — D, D — 25, 13

SLEEVE 2 PIECES — C, E, E — 30, 34

FRONT 2 PIECES — C', D, A, B' — 5, 22, 20

BACK — C', C², B', B² — 27, 40

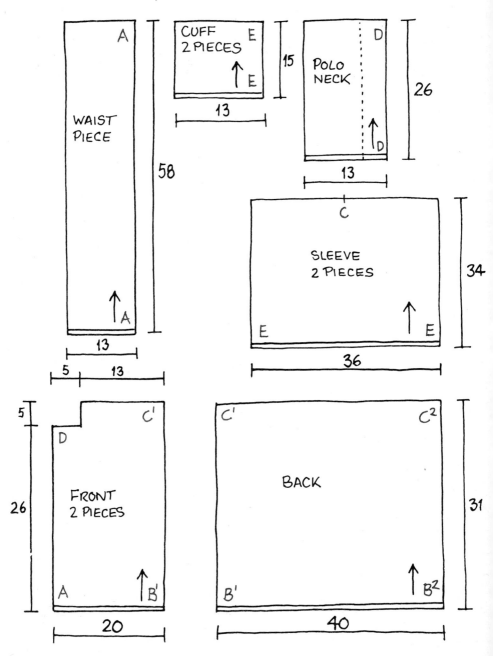

SIZE 10-12 YEARS

WAIST PIECE

A

58

13

5   13

CUFF
2 PIECES

E

E

13

15

POLO
NECK

D

D

26

13

SLEEVE
2 PIECES

C

E   E

36

34

5

D

FRONT
2 PIECES

C'

A   B'

26

20

C'   C²

BACK

B'   B²

40

31

SIZE 13-14 YEARS

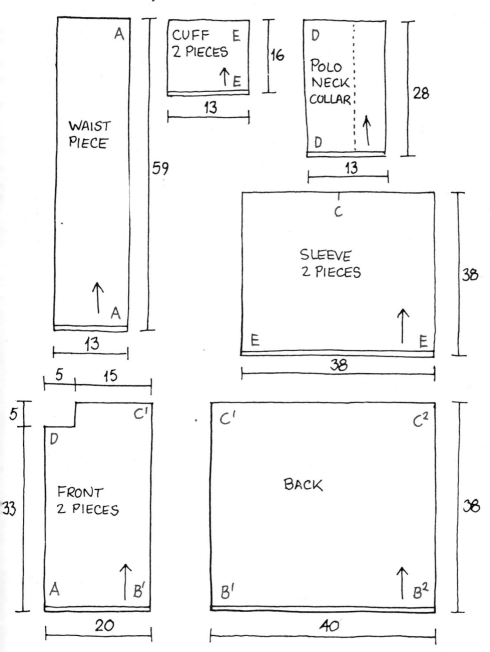

Jacket with hood

Size: Medium, women's size 14, men's 38–40.
Yarn: All types suitable. Thick yarn and no. 6 needles have been used for the jacket on pages 76–7.
Amount required: 18–22 × 50 g.
Note: The length of the jacket can be increased to make a full-length coat. Marks X–X on the pattern pieces show where to attach the inside pockets, which are optional.

Jacket with collar

The design is the same as before, but the hood is turned down to form
a collar 16 × 56 cm. Start with the short side – i.e. cast on 16 cm.

Sew all the garment pieces together. Then pick up the stitches on
the front edge and knit 5-cm-wide borders.

Knit a belt about 7 cm wide, long enough to tie comfortably in the
front.

JACKET

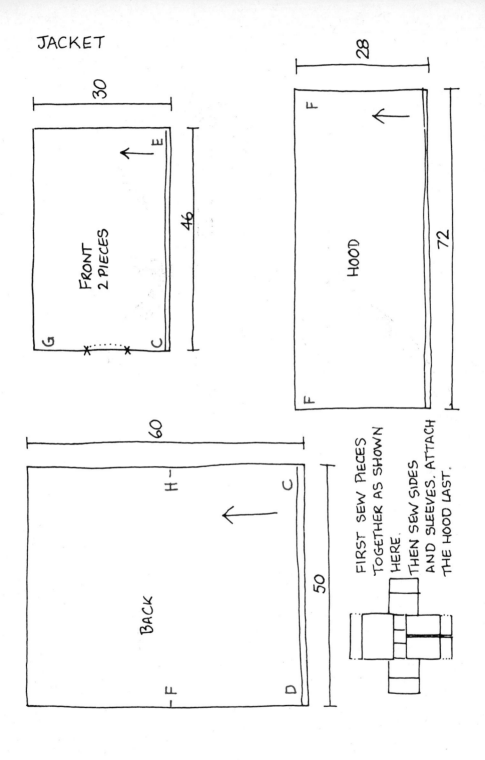

FRONT 2 PIECES — 30, 46 — E, G, C

BACK — 60, 50 — H, C, F, D

HOOD — 28, 72 — F, F

FIRST SEW PIECES TOGETHER AS SHOWN HERE.

THEN SEW SIDES AND SLEEVES. ATTACH THE HOOD LAST.

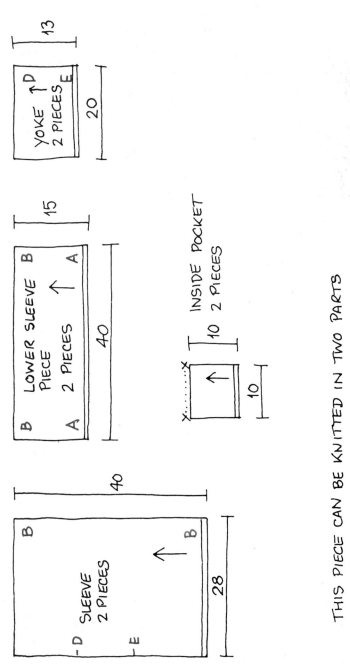

YOKE
2 PIECES
D
E
13
20

LOWER SLEEVE
PIECE
2 PIECES
A   B
B   A
15
40

INSIDE POCKET
2 PIECES
10
10

SLEEVE
2 PIECES
D   B
E   B
40
28

BOTTOM STRIP
G   H
15
120

THIS PIECE CAN BE KNITTED IN TWO PARTS

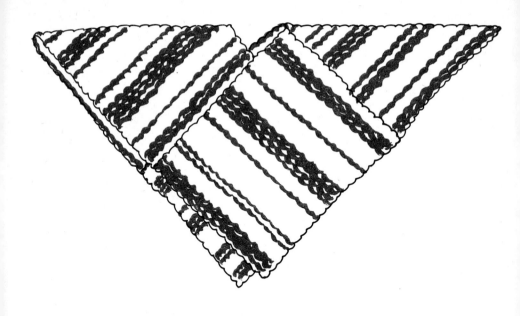

Poncho

Size: For adults. To alter the size see the marks a–b on the pattern which is the distance from the neck to the wrist.
Yarn: All types suitable. For best results, do not mix different qualities of yarn.
Amount required: About 20×50 g for the adult size.

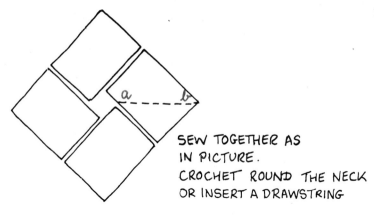

SEW TOGETHER AS
IN PICTURE.
CROCHET ROUND THE NECK
OR INSERT A DRAWSTRING

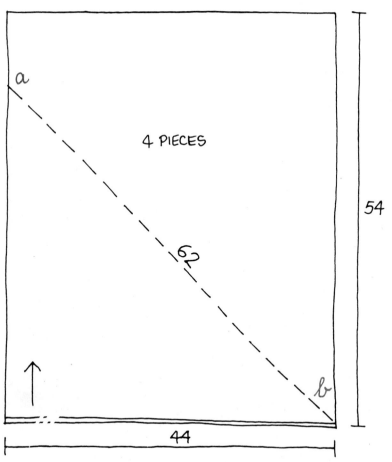

a

4 PIECES

54

62

b

44

Bags

The sizes on this pattern are only examples. You can change the measurements as you wish.

Yarn: Long strips of cloth, or the warp used for carpet-weaving, rope, and odds and ends of any yarn are suitable. The bag on page 17 has been knitted with fish netting grade 12/24 and with no. 4 needles. For the ball bag we recommend fish netting grade 12/9 and no. 0 needles.

Note: The bottoms of these bags and the knitted, straight handles should be strengthened with cloth or leather.

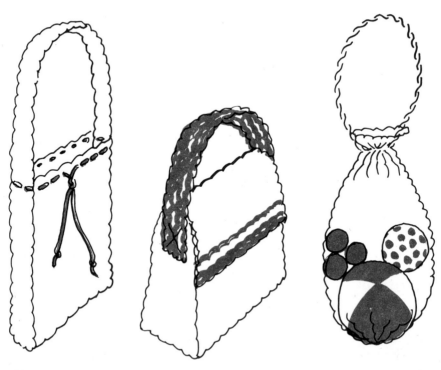

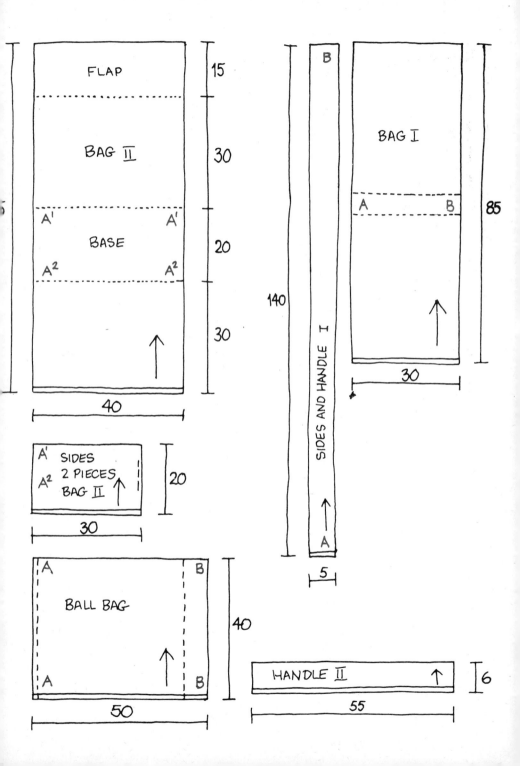

FLAP

BAG II

15

30

A'   A'

BASE

A²   A²

20

30

40

A'   SIDES

A²   2 PIECES

BAG II

20

30

A   B

BALL BAG

A   B

40

50

B

BAG I

A   B

85

30

140

SIDES AND HANDLE I

A

5

HANDLE II

6

55

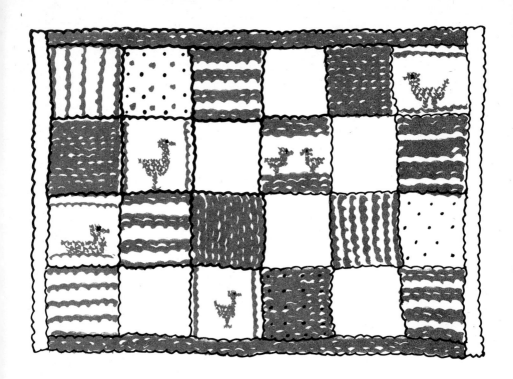

Odds and ends

Now you can put your own ideas into practice. Make squares and bands and sew them together for blankets, bedcovers, cushions or anything else you can think of! For decorations, see page 15.

Tops for everyone

Size: See chart on pages 92–3 for all sizes.
Yarn: All types suitable.
Special instructions: These tops are made out of six fabric pieces plus a hood. All these pieces can be started from either side I or II. All the other pieces, marked with red, must be cast on from side I for elasticity. The idea of these tops is to combine the pieces according to what sort of garment you want.

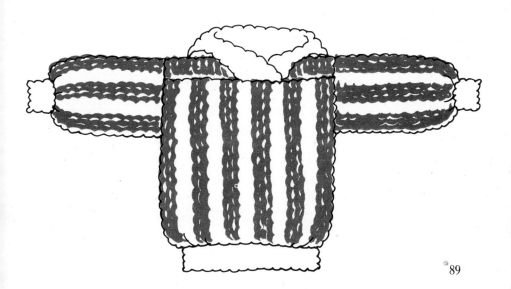

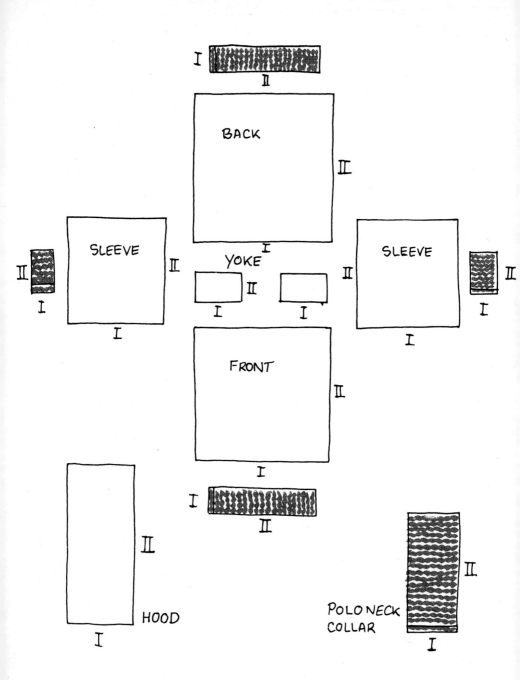

BACK

SLEEVE

YOKE

SLEEVE

FRONT

HOOD

POLO NECK COLLAR

Some notes about knitting

It is hard to say when the art of knitting first began or what garments it was used for.

There is a picture of women wearing some kind of socks in an Egyptian burial chamber dating from approximately 1900 B.C., and museums in Detroit and Basle have a few fragments of indigo and white cotton knitting bearing knitted inscriptions in old Arabic, originating probably from Egypt in the period 1171–800 B.C.

An impression of a stockinged foot was found in the lava which buried Pompeii in A.D. 79, and a child's sock from the third or fourth century has been found in Egypt.

Not much survives from the Middle Ages, but during the fifteenth century the art of knitting spread all over Europe. There is a painting in one of the museums in Hamburg of a Madonna knitting, and nuns in Naantali in Finland are known to have knitted socks. Silk stockings, made to measure, were given as a distinguished gift to many kings in the sixteenth century. The Swedish King Erik XIV, who loved splendour, imported a pair of silk stockings for himself, which cost him as much as he paid yearly to his royal shoemaker.

In Sweden the oldest surviving knitting by common people is a group of sweaters from Holland. They were usually knitted in one colour and decorated with purl stitches on the smooth side. Knitting made a significant contribution to the income of the people in this area where agriculture gave a poor livelihood.

Wool, being cheap, was usually the basic material for clothing. 'One basket of linen, four cloth coats, one red woollen jacket, one rough shirt, four pairs of trousers, two hats' was the list of clothes which a Gotland student took with him when he went to study in Uppsala.

Knitting came early to the coastal regions of Sweden and then spread inland. By the nineteenth century people had taken to wearing white stockings in fancy patterns which changed according to fashion year by year. Long knitting samples were made, some of which can be seen in museums, but which were often used up in making patchwork bedspreads.

Measurement chart (in cm)

AGE	SIZE			FRONT	BACK	ARMS
CHILDREN	CHILD'S HEIGHT: Head/heel			SIDES* I × II	SIDES* I × II	SIDES* I × II
approx. $\frac{1}{2}$ year	56			24 × 21	24 × 24	14 × 20
1	63			28 × 25	28 × 28	18 × 24
2	74			30 × 27	30 × 30	20 × 25
3	84			32 × 29	32 × 32	24 × 26
4	98			34 × 30	34 × 34	27 × 27
5	110			36 × 32	36 × 36	30 × 30
6	120			38 × 34	38 × 38	33 × 33
8	130			40 × 36	40 × 40	35 × 35
10	140			41 × 39	41 × 43	38 × 38
12	150			43 × 42	43 × 46	38 × 38
14	160			46 × 45	46 × 49	40 × 40
16	170			49 × 48	49 × 52	40 × 40
	UK	Continental	US			
Women	10	34	8	51 × 53	51 × 58	38 × 38
	12	36–38	10	53 × 55	53 × 60	39 × 39
	14	40–42	12	55 × 55	55 × 60	40 × 40
	16	44–46	14	58 × 55	58 × 60	40 × 40
Men	36	46	36	58 × 58	58 × 62	44 × 42
	38–40	48–50	38–40	60 × 60	60 × 64	46 × 44
	42–44	52–54	42–44	62 × 62	62 × 66	46 × 44
	46–48	56–58	46–48	64 × 64	64 × 68	48 × 44

*Sides I and II refer to diagrams on p. 90.

SHOULDER PIECE	HOOD	CUFF	HEM	POLO NECK
SIDES* I × II	SIDES* I × II	SIDES* I × II	SIDES* I × II	SIDES* I × II
8 × 4	17 × 42	3 × 11	3 × 16	—
9 × 5	18 × 44	4 × 11	4 × 18	—
10 × 5	20 × 48	4 × 11	4 × 20	—
10 × 5	21 × 50	5 × 12	5 × 22	—
12 × 6	22 × 53	5 × 12	5 × 24	12 × 30
12 × 6	23 × 56	6 × 12	6 × 26	14 × 31
13 × 7	24 × 59	6 × 13	6 × 28	14 × 32
14 × 7	24 × 62	6 × 13	6 × 30	14 × 32
14 × 7	25 × 64	6 × 13	6 × 30	14 × 33
15 × 8	25 × 66	7 × 13	7 × 32	16 × 33
17 × 9	26 × 68	7 × 14	7 × 32	16 × 34
18 × 9	26 × 70	7 × 14	7 × 34	16 × 34
20 × 10	26 × 70	7 × 14	7 × 34	16 × 34
20 × 10	26 × 70	7 × 14	7 × 34	16 × 35
21 × 11	27 × 70	7 × 14	7 × 38	16 × 35
21 × 11	27 × 70	7 × 14	7 × 40	16 × 36
22 × 11	28 × 72	7 × 14	7 × 40	16 × 36
22 × 11	28 × 72	7 × 15	7 × 40	16 × 36
24 × 12	30 × 73	7 × 16	7 × 41	17 × 37
24 × 12	30 × 73	7 × 16	7 × 42	17 × 38

Knitting needle sizes

UK	Metric	US
14	2 mm	00
13	$2\frac{1}{4}$ mm	0
12	$2\frac{3}{4}$ mm	1
11	3 mm	2
10	$3\frac{1}{4}$ mm	3
		4
9	$3\frac{3}{4}$ mm	5
8	4 mm	6
7	$4\frac{1}{2}$ mm	7
6	5 mm	8
5	$5\frac{1}{2}$ mm	9
4	6 mm	10
3	$6\frac{1}{2}$ mm	$10\frac{1}{2}$
2	7 mm	11
1	$7\frac{1}{2}$ mm	13
0	8 mm	
00	9 mm	
000	10 mm	

Clothes sizes

Women

UK	Continental	US
10	34	8
12	36–38	10
14	40–42	12
16	44–46	14

Men

UK and US	Continental
36	46
38–40	48–50
42–44	52–54
46–48	56–58

Metric and Imperial measurements approximate equivalents

10 mm = 1 cm, 100 cm = 1 m

Metric	Imperial
1 cm	$\frac{1}{2}$ in.
12 mm	$\frac{1}{2}$ in.
2 cm	$\frac{3}{4}$ in.
3 cm	$1\frac{1}{4}$ in.
4 cm	$1\frac{1}{2}$ in.
5 cm	2 in.
10 cm	4 in.
50 cm	20 in.
1 metre	39 in.

Imperial	Metric
$\frac{1}{2}$ in.	12 mm
1 in.	$2\frac{1}{2}$ cm
10 in.	25 cm
12 in.	30 cm
36 in.	91 cm
40 in.	101 cm